A Child's Introduction to BALLET

A Child's Introduction to
BALLET

The stories, music, and magic of classical dance

Laura Lee
Illustrated by Meredith Hamilton

BLACK DOG
& LEVENTHAL
PUBLISHERS
NEW YORK

ISBN-10: 1-57912-699-5
ISBN-13: 978-1-57912-699-5

Library of Congress Cataloging-in-Publication Data
on file at the offices of the publisher.

Cover and interiors: Sheila Hart Design, Inc.

Manufactured in China

Published by
Black Dog & Leventhal Publishers, Inc.
151 West 19th Street
New York, New York 10011

Distributed by
Workman Publishing Company
225 Varick Street
New York, NY 10014

g f e d c b a

AUTHOR'S ACKNOWLEDGMENTS

In ballet, everybody gets to take a bow. With books, only one or two names show up on the cover. It's not really fair. As my father often said, "When you see a turtle on a fence post, you know it didn't get there by itself." Please give a round of applause to the following people: my fearless editor, Laura Ross; Meredith Hamilton, who created the beautiful artwork; designer Sheila Hart; publisher J.P. Leventhal; production director True Sims; and copy editor Iris Bass, all of whom worked together to make me appear much smarter than I actually am.

Most of all, I would like to thank Valery Lantratov, the artistic director of the Russian National Ballet Foundation, for his help and advice in everything related to the ballet and for his friendship and support.

For Laura Ann and Laila—
who were always better at ballet than I.

MHH

Contents

Circus Polka

Peter and the Wolf

Fancy Free

Romeo and Juliet

Swan Lake

The Nutcracker

Coppélia

Welcome to the magical world of ballet!

The first time you see a ballet, it may look a little strange. Women are gliding around on the tips of their toes, their skirts stick out like the petals of a daisy, and both the men and women are wearing tights. No one talks. They tell a whole story through movements—and they leap and spin as if they might take off and start flying! How weird! And yet, somehow, it all looks elegant and beautiful. That's the magic of ballet.

In this book you'll read about how ballet came to be; how high dancers can leap. How they can spin so many times without getting dizzy; and what they have in common with pigeons, swans, and ducks. You'll meet many of the most famous and important ballet dancers and **choreographers** (the people who invent the dances). You'll even learn some ballet steps that you can do yourself.

Best of all, you'll read the stories of the world's greatest ballets—and, as the stories unfold, you can listen to pieces of music from some of them and start to become a ballet expert!

If you have taken a ballet class, you may have noticed that the words for ballet movements are in French. (If you haven't taken a ballet class, don't worry. We'll talk about some ballet words like **plié** (PLEE-ay), **jeté** (jet-TAY), and **pirouette** (pir-roo-ET) soon. One of the few terms that doesn't come from the French is the word "ballet" itself. It is from an Italian word, *ballare*—which just means "to dance."

The earliest ballets looked nothing like what we see on stage today. There were no **pointe shoes** or **tutus** (costumes with stiff skirts), and none of the basic positions or steps that they teach in today's ballet classes. And in the early days, no women were allowed! Instead, men dressed up as women and danced the female parts.

I am Natasha. When you see me, you know that there is some great music to play or a fun fact to learn. As you read each ballet story, I will direct you to the right track on the CD so you can listen and imagine the ballet unfolding before your eyes. Sometimes I'll tell you something interesting about the story or one of the ballet's creators.

It took another *three hundred years* before ballet started to resemble what we call "ballet" today.

Ballet was invented in Italy— though it became what it is today in France. The very first ballet may have been created in 1459 for an Italian royal wedding. At the banquet, the performers did dances representing the dishes being served. (Can you imagine a broccoli ballet?)

Italy 1400's

Ballet got a great boost in the 1700s, by **King Louis XIV** of France, who appeared on stage as a dancer and passed a royal decree encouraging other nobles to do the same. Louis founded the Paris Opéra Ballet in an old, abandoned tennis court (yes, people played tennis four hundred years ago!).

Louis's teacher was a man named **Pierre Beauchamp**, who in 1671 became the director of the first ballet training school, the Royal Academy of Dance, in Paris. Beauchamp was inspired to create ballets by the pigeons outside his window. He liked to feed them corn and watch as they ran to eat it. The different patterns the pigeons made gave him ideas for his dances. Pierre Beauchamp invented the concept of **turnout** and what we now call the **five classical positions** of the feet.

Listen to Track 1.
In the early days, **composers** did not write music specifically for ballet. Dances were performed to songs that were already popular, such as this court music. As you listen, imagine the noblemen and gentlewomen entertaining at court.

France 1700's

1900's

2000

The God of the Dance

Gaetano Vestris and his son, **Auguste**, were two of the most famous dancers from ballet's very early days. When they danced together in London in 1781, Parliament interrupted its session so that its members could see them.

Gaetano was pretty full of himself. He called himself the "God of the Dance" and once when a woman stepped on his foot he told her she'd put all of Paris into mourning. As rude and self-centered as he was offstage, no one was more regal or elegant onstage.

The only dancer who rivaled Gaetano was his son, Auguste, who was known for his astonishingly high leaps. One day, one of Auguste's admirers said to another, "How light he is! He must live on a diet of butterflies!"

Gaetano Vestris and Teresa Fogliazzi

"No," replied the other. "He eats only their wings."

Unfortunately, there was no video back then and no one had yet invented a system to record dance movements on paper, so we don't really know what the ballets of Gaetano, Auguste, and their contemporaries looked like. All that is left of the great dancers of the past are a few drawings and stories that have been passed down.

People sometimes say that when dancers are offstage they walk like ducks. This is because dancers train themselves from an early age to "turn out" their legs so their feet point away from each other.

Even grown-up dancers take class every day, and that is when they practice the basic positions and movements of ballet.

But why on earth would dancers want to walk like ducks? Simple. When the hips and legs are turned out, it is easier to change positions quickly and to move in different directions. Try it yourself. With your feet facing forward, move to the left and the right. You have to make a little turn before you can change direction. Now rotate your hips outward with your feet pointing away from each other and your heels touching. Move to the left and the right. It's easier, isn't it?

When your legs are turned out, you can also lift them higher than you can with your feet turned forward. (Try this, too.)

Once you've mastered turnout, you're ready to move on to the basics—what are known as the five classic ballet positions. The five positions are the first thing a dancer must master. You can try them now, using the directions on the next page. Look at the pictures to see how your arms should look!

What a Pain!

In the eighteenth century, somebody invented a machine called a "hip turner" to force the hips to turn out. Why don't we use it today? Well, it turns out it was not very good at creating turnout. What it *did* do was injure the dancers' knees and ankles. Yow!

THE FIVE POSITIONS

First Position Stand straight, your heels touching, your toes pointed outward as far as they can go sideways, starting from all the way up at your hips.

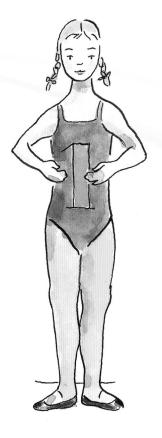

Listen to Track 2.
During at least part of almost every ballet class, the dancers stand at a ballet **barre** (just a fancy French way of saying "bar"—a long rod they hold onto). The ballet master or teacher plays music like this while the dancers stretch and warm up. Sometimes a piano player is right in the room, playing live music at the teacher's request.

Second Position Start in First Position. Slide one foot straight out to the side and point your foot. Then lower your heel so that it lines up with the other one and your body is centered above them.

Tackling Something New

The Dallas Cowboys' great running back, Herschel Walker, once danced with the Fort Worth Ballet Company. Walker said there wasn't that much difference between tackling football players and performing pirouettes. He said that ballet was every bit as tough and demanding as football, but that he had to use "a completely different set of muscles."

And finally...

Fifth Position Start in Fourth Position and then bring your right foot in close to your left, so that your right heel is in front of your left big toe and your toes are still pointing straight out to the sides. This is a little tricky until you develop your turnout. And it's a little bit hard to balance—which is why dancers sometimes use the barre to steady themselves when they are learning and practicing.

Third Position From Second Position, bring your right foot in front of your left so that the heel of the right touches the middle of the left foot. Your toes should still be pointing outward.

Fourth Position From Third Position, slide your right foot forward until your heel is a little way in front of your left big toe. Keep your toes pointed away from each other.

Now you know the basic ballet positions!

La Fille Mal Gardée
(The Badly Guarded Girl)

Original Choreography: Jean Dauberval
Music: Originally, various composers; 1828, Ferdinand Hérold
First performed Paris 1789

The oldest ballet still being performed to this day, *La Fille Mal Gardée* is the story of a lively girl named Lisette.

Lisette is an only child and so clever and spirited that everyone warns her mother, Madame Simone, that Lisette needs to be watched carefully!

Mother and daughter live on a large farm. Lisette loves Colin, a handsome but poor farmhand. Her mother would never approve of Colin, so Lisette doesn't dare spend much time with him.

One day Madame Simone catches Lisette talking to Colin, and she is furious! She fires Colin immediately, and decides then and there that it is time for Lisette to wed someone else.

It happens that next door is a farm belonging to a wealthy widower, Thomas, father of a boy named Alain. The neighbors agree that their children should marry. But Lisette does not like Alain, who is a silly boy more interested in chasing butterflies than in marriage.

On the day the wedding is supposed to take place, there is a storm and it must be postponed. To keep Lisette away from Colin, Madame Simone orders her to stay in the house. Lisette notices Colin peeking through the window and she comes up with a plan to distract her mother. She asks Madame Simone to play the tambourine so she can practice her dancing. Soon Lisette's mother becomes tired and falls asleep.

Poets have written many beautiful words trying to explain what dance is. The eighteenth-century ballet master P. Rameau was not poetic at all. He said, "Dancing is no more than knowing how to bend and straighten the knees at the proper time."

As soon as she does, Colin sneaks into the house and asks Lisette to marry him. Just then, her mother starts to wake up and Colin hides in the hayloft —but he accidentally leaves a scarf behind.

When Madame Simone finds the scarf she knows that Colin has been there. She doesn't know where he is hiding so she decides to lock Lisette in the hayloft for safekeeping! "Don't come out until you're ready to get married," Lisette's mother tells her.

Lisette comes out wearing her best dress—and holding Colin's hand. Colin begs Lisette's mother for her daughter's hand, and when Madame Simone sees how much they love each other, she cannot help but agree to the marriage. The wedding takes place after all, and Lisette and Colin live happily ever after.

DRESSED FOR SUCCESS

Can you imagine dancing in a heavy dress, bulky shoes, and a huge powdered wig? That was the way it was done until the 1700s, when a Belgian dancer named **Marie-Anne Cupis de Camargo** shortened her skirt so people could see her fancy footwork. It was only short enough to show her ankles but still, people were shocked!

In the 1800s, dancers started wearing **"romantic tutus,"** long, fluffy, lightweight skirts. These became shorter and shorter and a lot stiffer until they stuck straight out. This is called a **"classic tutu."**

Marie-Anne

before

after

> ### Daring Mr. Leotard
>
> The leotard you probably wear in dance class was named for a French trapeze artist named **Jules Leotard**. The song "The Daring Young Man on the Flying Trapeze" was written about him.

La Sylphide

Original Choreography: Filippo Taglioni
Original Music: Jean Schneitzhoeffer
First performed: Paris, 1832
New Music: Herman Severin Løvenskiold
New Choreography: August Bournonville
First performed: Copenhagen, Denmark, 1836

La Sylphide takes place in old Scotland. A young man named James is trying to sleep in a large chair by a blazing fireplace. It is the night before his wedding, and James is dressed in the traditional Scottish wedding costume, a man's skirt called a kilt.

James dreams of a beautiful fairy, a "sylphide." At the same time, Gurn is dreaming of Effie, James's fiancée, because he is secretly in love with her.

James wakes up, and sees the sylphide in front of him! He reaches out for her but she disappears into the fireplace in a puff of smoke. James is confused. Was she real or just a dream? He is still thinking about this when his mother enters the room with Effie. They get to work planning the big wedding. As the bridesmaids arrive, Gurn asks them to tell Effie to call off the wedding, but they ignore him.

The girls ask the village witch, Old Madge, to tell Effie's fortune. Effie asks Old Madge if her marriage will be happy. "Oh yes," says the old woman. "You will be very happy in marriage."

"So…James loves me?" Effie asks.

Old Madge shakes her head. "No," she says.

James chases the old woman away with a broom, but he can't stop thinking about the sylphide. The fairy reappears but this time she looks sad. She tells James that she is in love with someone who does not love her in return. He kisses her.

Gurn has been watching the whole time, and he runs up the stairs to tell Effie that he saw James kissing somebody else. Effie ridicules Gurn for jealously making up stories.

Don't get confused! There is another ballet with a name that sounds like *La Sylphide*. *Les Sylphides* was created almost 100 years after *La Sylphide*, to music by Frédéric Chopin. *Les Sylphides* has beautiful fairies (sylphs) but no story at all.

The wedding goes on as planned but when James starts to slip the ring on Effie's finger, the sylphide darts in and grabs it. The guests are shocked when the ring disappears. The fairy tells James that she will die if he marries someone else. To prevent such a tragedy he follows her, leaving Effie crying at the altar. Gurn rushes in to comfort her.

James follows the sylphide into an enchanted forest, but every time he tries to reach her she disappears. Old Madge agrees to help James by giving him a magic scarf. If he puts it around the fairy's shoulders, her wings will fall off and she will not be able to fly away again.

James runs to the sylphide and puts the scarf around her shoulders. But when her wings fall off, she falls dead at his feet. Old Madge has tricked him! James is filled with grief as a group of sylphides carries his love off to the heavens.

In the distance wedding bells ring for Gurn and Effie.

GET THE POINTE?

Sure, leaps and spins are impressive, but one of the hardest things a ballerina (female ballet dancer) does is stand still. A ballerina on the very tips of her toes in her pointe shoes has to balance all her weight on a spot only a little larger than one square inch across. She needs to have excellent balance!

Try standing on one foot...it's not really too hard once you get the hang of it. Now try standing on one foot on ordinary tiptoe. It's harder. Now imagine standing on the very tips of your toes, in a special, close-fitting shoe with a hard tip. THAT takes a lot of practice!

For many years dancers performed this feat in regular, soft shoes, and they just couldn't stay **en pointe** for very long. Then someone invented special shoes with hard toes—made by stiffening the fabric with glue—which made dancing on one's toes a little more comfortable. But not THAT comfortable. A ballerina's toes are often bruised and sore. And sometimes, in a quiet ballet, you can hear the toes of the shoes clomping!

Why don't men dance en pointe? Are their feet too big? No. Men could dance that way but they usually don't. It's a tradition. There's no other reason.

Twinkle Toes

A ballerina named Marie Taglioni made dancing en pointe popular. Marie became famous in the 1830s when her father, Filippo Taglioni, created the ballet *La Sylphide* for her. To create the illusion that she was a weightless fairy, Marie danced on the tips of her toes.

After Marie's last performance, the audience was so sad to see her go that a chef cooked her ballet slipper and her most devoted admirers ate it!

Giselle

Original Choreography: Jean Coralli and Jules Perrot
Music: Adolphe Adam
First performed: Paris, 1841

The story of *Giselle* takes place a long time ago, in a little village in France, where a pretty girl named Giselle lives with her mother and dreams of marrying a boy named Loys. Giselle has been interested in Loys ever since he came to town, which annoys the local gamekeeper, Hilarion, who is in love with Giselle himself. What neither of them know is that Loys is actually a count in disguise.

One day Loys stops by and Giselle dances with him until her mother orders her into the house.

Hilarion is so jealous that he decides to break into Loys's house. There, he discovers a long velvet cloak and a silver sword. As he is trying to figure out what they mean, a trumpet sounds and he is forced to hide.

Giselle is one of the few ballets from the 1800s that has been performed continually since it was created. One of the reasons it has stayed popular is that the main character is a juicy and challenging acting role for a ballerina. Giselle begins as an innocent and happy girl, has her heart broken, goes mad, and is finally reborn as a spirit. To play Giselle a ballerina needs to create many different moods for the audience.

Listen to Track 3.

Giselle was one of the first ballets that had music written especially for it. The composer created a melody or theme for each character, and these themes appear throughout the ballet to help you hear how the characters are feeling. Listen to the theme that plays when Giselle first enters. How do you think she is feeling when this music is playing?

A party of noblemen rides into town, and Giselle and her mother greet them. Giselle has never before seen people with such elegant gowns and beautiful jewelry. She dances for and entertains the guests. After they have gone, Loys returns and Giselle begins to tell him about the party. Just then Hilarion enters and thrusts the silver sword between them. He has figured out Loys's secret.

The crest on the sword matches the royal crest on a hunting horn left by one of the nobles. "He's not a peasant!" Hilarion exclaims, and to prove it, he blows the horn. The nobles answer its call. He is really Count Albrecht and he is engaged to marry someone else!

Giselle is grief-stricken. She collapses into her mother's arms and dies!

A few nights later, deep in a dark forest, the Queen of the Wilis emerges from the shadows to summon her subjects. Wilis are the spirits of girls who have been abandoned by men who had promised to marry them. Every night they rise from their graves to seek revenge by forcing any man they can find to dance until he dies of exhaustion. Giselle's spirit has come to join them.

Hilarion comes into the woods and is made to dance until he dies.

That very evening Count Albrecht visits Giselle's grave. When the Queen of the Wilis demands that he dance, Giselle dances instead, and then he dances with her. He grows more and more tired but, thanks to the power of Giselle's love, Albrecht survives the night. In the morning, Giselle leaves Albrecht a lily and fades away, never to be seen again.

THE LANGUAGE OF BALLET—IT'S FRENCH!

If you want to be a dancer, you have to know at least a little bit of French, but that's a fun thing to learn. Here are some words that every ballet student knows, along with a lesson in how to do the movement it describes. There are lots of other ballet words in the glossary at the end of the book.

Battement tendu (batt-mahn tan-doo) Slide one foot away from your body, to the front, side, or back, and then back to its original position. This warms and stretches the feet.

Attitude (att-ee-tood) In ballet, "attitude" is a good thing! Lift one leg so that it stretches out behind you with its knee bent, keeping your leg turned out.

Développé (duh-veh-loh-pay) Développé means "develop"—did you guess that? It is a move that "develops." Standing in one of the five positions, you bend one leg to bring your big toe up toward your other knee—and then you unfold the leg and raise your foot up high, to the front, side, or back, until the bent leg is out straight.

Arabesque (ara-besk) This is a classic movement that you will see hundreds of times when watching any ballet. Start by balancing on one leg and then stretch your other leg straight out behind you, as high as you can without bending it. (This one has special arm positions, too.)

Plié (plee-ay) Stand in either First or Second Position and bend at the knees, holding your knees out sideways over your feet. When doing pliés in second position, your heels should stay on the floor. When doing a deep plié in first position, your heels have to pop up.

Take a Leap!

Professional male dancers can leap somewhere between four and five feet off the ground. That's probably taller than you are. Some of the great leapers, like **Mikhail Baryshnikov** (mee-KAYL bar-ISH-nee-koff) when he was at his best, could jump as high as six feet—right over the head of a full-grown man! Male dancers jump slightly higher than female dancers. How long can a person stay in the air? Not long. Basketball star Michael Jordan, one of the greatest leapers in the world of sports, could stay in the air only a little bit less than a second. Great dancers can do about the same.

Jeté (jzeh-tay) The word "jeté" means "thrown," and to perform a jeté you THROW yourself in the air in a leap from one foot to the other. A *grand jeté* is a big jump forward.

Coppélia

Original Choreography: Arthur Saint-Léon, based on a story by E. T. A. Hoffmann
Music: Léo Delibes
First performed: Paris, 1870
Best-known choreography: Marius Petipa, 1884

In a small village lives an old inventor named Dr. Coppélius and his "daughter," Coppélia. Every day, the girl sits on her balcony reading a book but she never says a thing. Even the friendliest girl in the town, Swanilda, can't get Coppélia to talk.

Listen to Track 4.

Before he composed the music of Coppélia, Léo Delibes took a walking trip in Hungary. He was inspired by the folk music and dancing of the region. He took notes and wrote a mazurka, a lively folk dance, which he included in the ballet. Does it make you want to get up and dance?

One day Swanilda goes looking for her boyfriend, Franz, and finds him gazing up at Coppélia and blowing kisses to her. Swanilda runs away in tears.

That night, when Dr. Coppélius goes for his evening walk he loses his house key. Swanilda picks up the key and convinces her girlfriends that they should go up and try to meet Coppélia face to face. As they make their plans, Franz sneaks up to Coppélia's balcony using a ladder.

When the girls tiptoe into the doctor's workshop, they see dolls and doll-making equipment everywhere. And there is Coppélia, behind a curtain, sitting in her usual chair, reading a book. Swanilda begins to laugh. She now understands why the inventor's "daughter" never answers her: Coppélia is a doll! The girls wind up all the dolls and watch them dance, but Dr. Coppélius arrives and shoos them out. Swanilda stays—behind Coppélia's curtain.

Franz climbs in through the window. When he sees the inventor, he explains that he wishes to marry his "daughter." Dr. Coppélius asks Franz to have a drink with him and slips a potion into Franz's cup that makes him fall fast asleep.

You may remember that when ballet was first performed, only men were allowed to dance professionally. By the time of Coppélia *(cop-PAYL-ya), though, everything had changed and ballerinas were the big stars. The role of Franz in* Coppélia *was often danced by a woman dressed as a man.*

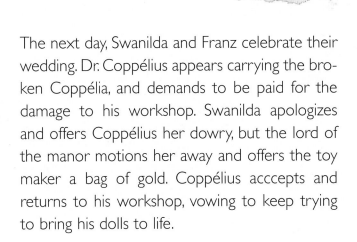

Listen to Track 5.

After Swanilda discovers that Coppélia is really a doll, the girls play with the wind-up toys and make them dance. Listen to some of the music and imagine how a dancer might move like a wind-up toy. You can even try it yourself!

While Franz sleeps, Coppélius looks in his books of spells for the one that will bring Coppélia to life. He follows some instructions and, to his amazement, Coppélia begins to move. What he does not realize is that this is really Swanilda wearing Coppélia's dress. One by one, Swanilda winds up all the dolls in the workshop. When the doctor is completely distracted, she pulls Franz toward the door and they run out of the house.

It is only then that Coppélius pulls back the curtains and sees the limp body of Coppélia, who never came to life after all.

The next day, Swanilda and Franz celebrate their wedding. Dr. Coppélius appears carrying the broken Coppélia, and demands to be paid for the damage to his workshop. Swanilda apologizes and offers Coppélius her dowry, but the lord of the manor motions her away and offers the toy maker a bag of gold. Coppélius acccepts and returns to his workshop, vowing to keep trying to bring his dolls to life.

The Russians Are Coming!

So far we've been reading mostly about ballets that were created in France. From now on we'll be reading about a lot of ballets and dancers from Russia. Russians were involved in ballet almost from the beginning, just not very seriously involved.

Things changed dramatically when a Frenchman named Marius Petipa came to Russia in 1840.

Petipa gave male dancers more to do. Instead of just propping up the ballerinas, the men in Petipa's ballets leaped, spun, and got to be the center of attention sometimes. But the beautiful ballerinas in flowing white were still the stars.

Petipa produced more than sixty ballets, including some that are still performed regularly to this day. In fact, the three most popular ballets in the world—*The Nutcracker*, *Swan Lake*, and *Sleeping Beauty*—were all choreographed by Petipa and his assistant Lev Ivanov, to music by the great composer **Peter Ilyich Tchaikovsky** (chai-KOFF-ski).

Q. What famous ballet company was originally made up entirely of orphans?

A. Moscow's Bolshoi Ballet.

In 1773, the council for the Moscow Orphanage offered a salary and bonus to former dancer **Fillippo Beccari** if he could train the young boys and girls to be dancers. Beccari must have been a GREAT teacher! Out of sixty-two children, he produced twenty-four **soloists**. From this group of talented orphans Russia's Bolshoi Ballet was born. Czar Alexander I awarded the company Imperial status in 1806, and the Bolshoi (this word means "big") is still one of the greatest ballet companies in the world—but of course it is not made up of orphans anymore.

One of Petipa's creations was the **divertissement** (di-vert-ees-mahn). (Yep, French again, even though we're in Russia now.) The word means "diversion" or "entertainment." Divertissements are scenes that break away from the main story of a ballet to showcase different kinds of dance. ("We now interrupt this story for some dance from Spain...")

Listen to track 6.
Does it sound familiar?
The "Sabre Dance" has been used in movies, TV shows, commercials, even at the circus! Maybe this is because it sounds so exciting.

The Music Lives On

There are some composers whose ballet music is rarely heard when there are no dancers around. Then there are other composers whose ballet music becomes very well known even though the original ballets are forgotten.

The "Sabre Dance" was written by **Aram Khachaturian** (ah-ram CATCH-a-TUR-i-an) for his 1942 ballet *Gayane*. You may never have a chance to see *Gayane*, but it's hard not to *hear* the "Sabre Dance."

Don Quixote

Original Choreography: Marius Petipa
Music: Leon Minkus
First performed: Moscow, 1869

Listen to Track 7.

Don Quixote was the first ballet Leon Minkus composed for **Marius Petipa**. Listen to this track and later compare it to the music you'll hear by other Russian composers. It is the music that plays when Don Quixote first sees Kitri and believes she is a beautiful princess.

Don Quixote is an old man who is so taken with stories of medieval knights that he starts to believe he is a real knight himself, traveling around with his trusty servant, Sancho Panza, in search of grand adventures.

In the ballet version of the story, Don Quixote arrives in a market square where he meets Kitri, the daughter of an innkeeper. Even though Kitri is in love with a young man named Basil, her father has offered her hand in marriage to the rich Gamache.

When Don Quixote sees Kitri he believes she is his beloved Dulcinea, a beautiful princess, and that Gamache is his rival for her affections. He challenges Gamache to a duel but the villagers just laugh at him.

Meanwhile, Basil has come up with a way to marry Kitri. He pretends he is dying and that his final wish is to marry her. As soon as Kitri's father gives his permission, Basil hops up from his "sickbed," perfectly healthy.

All the while, Don Quixote is out in the woods. When he sees a traveling puppet show, he thinks the puppets are enemy soldiers and engages them in battle. The wounded "knight" then takes a nap and dreams of his Dulcinea. Upon waking, he decides to march to the Duke's castle. There, he is challenged to a duel by the Knight of the Silver Moon (really his friend Carrasco), who finally convinces the old man to hang up his sword.

Swan Lake

Original choreography: J. W. Reisinger
Music: Peter Ilyich Tchaikovsky
First performed: Moscow, 1877
Best-known choreography: Marius Petipa

The story of *Swan Lake* begins on the birthday of Prince Siegfried. All of the nobles are gathered at the palace for a grand party. Siegfried's mother, the queen, gives the prince a gift of a crossbow and reminds him that he is now old enough to choose a bride. He dances with several beautiful women but none of them please him—so he takes his new crossbow to a nearby lake, to hunt.

Siegfried is about to shoot a bird when he sees that the creature is actually a beautiful woman. Odette, the Swan Queen, has been enchanted by an evil magician, the Baron von Rothbart. By day, she and her friends are swans but, between midnight and dawn, they return to their human form. The curse can only be broken by a man's true love.

The prince is enchanted with the beautiful Odette and he declares his love as the sun comes up and the women change back into swans.

Listen to Track 8.
Different variations of the Swan Theme can be heard throughout the ballet. This is the theme that plays as Odette and the swans swim on Swan Lake, one of the most famous pieces of ballet music ever. The challenge is for the ballerinas to perform their movements just as gracefully as a beautiful swan would.

Listen to Track 9.
When Odile dances for Siegfried and he believes her to be Odette, the Swan Theme returns—but it is not the same. Can you describe the differences?

Although it is now the one of most popular classical ballets in the world, Swan Lake's premiere was a complete flop! Critics and audiences hated it. Even Tchaikovsky, its composer, never thought much of Swan Lake, and he never lived to see a full production. A year after Tchaikovsky's death, Marius Petipa rechoreographed it into the ballet we still enjoy to this day.

Siegfried goes back to the palace, where the Queen reminds her son that he must choose a bride. In a series of *divertissements* (remember those?), dancers from Hungary, Poland, Spain, and Naples perform for him but he is not impressed.

Then a mysterious man arrives. The prince does not realize that he is the evil Baron von Rothbart in disguise. The man presents his daughter, Odile, and the prince is tricked into believing that she is Odette, his beloved Swan Queen.

Siegfried immediately proposes marriage and at that moment Rothbart reveals that it was all a trick to make Siegfried break his vow to Odette. She will have to stay a swan forever!

Back at the lake, Odette is grieving. As the other swans try to comfort her, Siegfried rushes to her side. He asks for her forgiveness and they agree never to be parted again—but just then the evil Baron von Rothbart appears.

Odette would rather die than remain enchanted forever, so she throws herself from the rocks. Siegfried cannot bear to lose her a second time so he follows her into the lake. In death, the power of their love defeats Rothbart and destroys his magic. The spell is lifted and the swans became maidens once again.

Mixed-up Swans

Why couldn't the prince tell Odette from Odile? Because they're danced by the same ballerina. In the original ballet, two different dancers performed the roles. Marius Petipa came up with the idea of having one ballerina dance both. It makes the prince's confusion more believable, but it makes the playing the part of Odette/Odile VERY challenging.

SUPER SPINNERS!

Pierina Legnani, the Italian ballerina who first danced the part of Odette/Odile in Marius Petipa's 1895 version of *Swan Lake*, performed thirty-two **fouettés** (FOO-eh-tays) in a row! Now every ballerina who performs Odile has to do the same. The audience expects it and keeps score, so sometimes the dancer mixes in other kinds of pirouettes to add to the excitement. *Fouetté* is a French word for "whip." In ballet, a fouetté is a quick whipping movement of the leg followed by a pirouette, or spin. In fact, Legnani had performed that same feat two years earlier, in Petipa's *Cinderella*, but it was in *Swan Lake* that the thirty-two fouettés stuck.

The world record for pirouettes is held by **Rowena Jackson** of New Zealand, who did 121 in a row in 1940. I bet she had a hard time walking a straight line after that!

Maybe you're wondering: how a ballerina can spin thirty-two times in a row without getting dizzy and falling down? Dancers have a trick for this.

First of all, you need to know what causes that dizzy feeling when you spin around. You get dizzy when your eyes and ears can't agree on whether you are standing still or moving. Your balance is controlled by three fluid-filled chambers deep inside your ear. When the fluid in the chambers stays calm and level, you feel fine.

But if you spin too much, the liquid inside your ears starts spinning really fast too, and it takes awhile for it to slow down and stop (just like when you stir your milk with a spoon and it keeps spinning around even when you take the spoon away). So your body may stop moving but the fluid keeps on going. Your eyes tell you you're standing still but your ears are telling your brain that you are moving. Your poor, confused brain doesn't know what to think, and you feel dizzy.

So how can a dancer do all those pirouettes without falling over? The trick they use is called "spotting." You can do it, too. Choose one spot on the wall, somewhere near eye level, to focus on. Then, start spinning around, but instead of keeping your head in line with your body, focus your eyes on that one spot for as long as you can before whipping your head around quickly to focus on the same spot again. This helps reduce dizziness because your head is staying still as long as possible and the fluid in your ears doesn't go into a big spin.

Sleeping Beauty

Original Choreography: Marius Petipa
Music: Peter Ilyich Tchaikovsky
First performed: Saint Petersburg, 1890

Once upon a time a beautiful princess is born and all the fairies of the kingdom are invited to a grand celebration. A scary old witch named Carabosse storms into the hall. Carabosse is very, very mad that she wasn't invited to the party.

She tells the king and queen that, when Aurora is sixteen, she will prick her finger and die. Fortunately, the Lilac Fairy has not yet given the baby her gift. She can't reverse the evil spell but she uses her powers to soften it. When Aurora pricks her finger, the Lilac Fairy says, she will not die. She will only fall asleep. When a handsome prince kisses her the spell will be broken.

Fairy tales make great ballets. One of the most famous ballets based on a fairy tale is Sleeping Beauty, *based on the tale of the French writer* **Charles Perrault.** *(I'm sure you know the story by heart, and the ballet version sticks pretty close to the way you have heard it.) It is also important because it was the first successful ballet set to music by the great composer Peter Ilyich Tchaikovsky.*

Dancing Ever After

In the audience for one production of *Sleeping Beauty* **was an eight-year-old girl named Anna Pavlova. She loved the ballet so much that she decided then and there she wanted to be a ballerina. You'll read more about Anna later—she became one of the greatest dancers ever.**

After the celebration the king issues a decree banning every sharp object from the kingdom and Aurora grows into a beautiful young woman.

On her sixteenth birthday, Aurora and her friends and family gather for a party at the palace. An old woman that Aurora does not recognize offers her a bouquet of flowers. As Aurora admires them she feels a pinch in her finger. Carabosse has hidden a sharp spindle in the flowers! Immediately Aurora falls into a deep sleep, and so does everybody else in the palace.

Many years go by as the entire kingdom sleeps. In a nearby forest, a prince named Florimund is hunting with his friends. The Lilac Fairy appears and shows Florimund a vision of Aurora. He falls in love at first sight and sets out to find the princess.

At long last he comes to a dark palace overgrown with vines and cobwebs It seems at first that no one lives in this strange place—but then he notices the beautiful woman of his vision. She is lying in bed, as still as death. The prince is overcome with her beauty. He bends down to kiss Aurora and when he does, she wakes up. The spell is broken.

Everyone celebrates at the beautiful wedding of Aurora and Florimund, surrounded by all sorts of magical fairy tale creatures. And of course everybody lives happily ever after.

Listen to Track 10.

The wedding scene in *Sleeping Beauty* features dances by different fairy-tale characters, including Puss in Boots, the Bluebird, and Little Red Riding Hood. Tchaikovsky created musical themes for each of the different characters and this one is the cat's theme. See if you can hear the "meow" the instruments make. Then **listen to Track 11**, which is the theme music for a very different creature. Can you imagine what it might be?

A: The Bluebird.

How Many Can YOU Do?

The Dance of the Bluebird in *Sleeping Beauty* is short but it is one of the hardest solos for a male dancer. He has to leap high, turn quickly, and cross and uncross his feet very fast. These movements are called **entrechats** (ON-tra-shahs).

A single midair entrechat is hard enough. Marie Camargo was the first dancer to do two in a row—that's four crosses all together. Because she wanted the freedom to do this tricky move she decided to shorten her skirts, and this began to change the traditional ballet costume forever.

Vaslav Nijinsky (vahs-LAHV Ni-ZJIN-ski) (we'll read more him about soon) was the only dancer who could do five entrechats, or ten movements in all. His record was broken in 1973 by **Wayne Sleep**, principal dancer of England's Royal Ballet, who performed six complete entrechats—twelve crosses—on a BBC television broadcast.

Wayne liked going for world's records. On November 28, 1988, he did 158 *grand jetés* in two minutes.

The Nutcracker

Original choreography: Lev Ivanov
(based on Marius Petipa's adaptation of a story by E. T. A. Hoffmann)
Music: Peter Ilych Tchaikovsky
First performed: Saint Petersburg, 1892

The story of *The Nutcracker* starts out on Christmas Eve at the home of the Stahlbaums. The family is holding a lavish party. The ladies dance in their colorful dresses and the gentlemen in their finest jackets, but young Marie is waiting for one guest in particular, her godfather, Drosselmeier.

Some people are frightened of Drosselmeier, but not Marie. She thinks he is clever and mysterious, and oh, what magical gifts he brings! Handcrafted wind-up toys, trains, soldiers, and spinning dolls.

This year, he brings the most wonderful gift of all, a wooden nutcracker. Marie skips off to bed that night with the nutcracker tucked safely under her arm. But just as she is drifting off to sleep she hears a sound.

Peeking out over the top of her blanket, Marie sees a giant mouse rising out of the floor with an entire mouse army behind him.

Just then, the nutcracker sits upright, throws off his blanket and leaps from the bed. He draws his wooden sword and raises it above his head.

In the original *Nutcracker* story the little girl is called Marie. Sometimes she goes by the Russian name Masha or the more American-sounding Clara.

The Nutcracker *is a Christmas holiday favorite and the most popular ballet in America. There are more than 2,000 performances of it every year around the country. You will probably have a chance to see it someday—and maybe even dance in it yourself, since it has lots of roles for young dancers.*

The nutcracker and a battalion of toy soldiers battle the Mouse King. Although the nutcracker fights bravely, the mouse knocks him down. Marie takes off her slipper and throws it at the mouse, who is startled long enough for the nutcracker to recover and win the battle.

While Marie is still catching her breath, Drosselmeier appears and reveals the secret of his Christmas present. The nutcracker is actually a handsome prince, and Marie's love for him has broken the spell. The prince takes Marie on a journey through the snow, to a magical kingdom where people from all nations take turns showing off their own special dances. It is all so perfect…but even the most beautiful dream must end. The next morning Marie wakes up with her wooden nutcracker beside her.

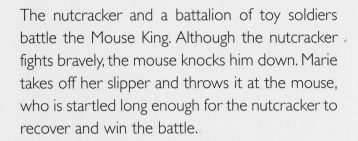

Listen to Track 12.
The second act of *The Nutcracker* features dances by people from different nations. This is the music for the Chinese variation. Does the music sound "Chinese" to you?
Listen to Track 13.
Marius Petipa asked Tchaikovsky to make the music for the Sugar Plum Fairy sound like the sprays of a fountain. To do this Tchaikovsky used a brand-new instrument, the celesta. It is played like a piano but when the keys are struck, the hammers inside hit little metal bars instead of strings.
Does it sound like a fountain?

Ballet to Go

Until the early part of the twentieth century, Russian ballet was thriving but people outside of Russia didn't hear much about it—until a man named **Sergei Diaghilev** (ser-GAY Dee-AH-gih-lev) founded a company called the **Ballets Russes**. What's strange is that the Ballets Russes never performed in Russia. Instead, it traveled around introducing ballet to the rest of us.

Diaghilev wasn't a dancer or a choreographer. He was a theatrical producer—an **impresario**—part showman and part businessman. Diaghilev assembed his company from the dancers of the imperial theaters of Russia, mostly during the time when they weren't performing at home, and took them to Paris.

Their long tours were hard. Sometimes there wasn't enough money to pay them. But, thanks to Diaghilev and his touring ballet dancers, many Americans saw professional ballet for the first time.

When Diaghilev died, in 1929, the Ballets Russes died with him. Yet his influence was felt around the world for many years to come.

Dying Swan

Choreography: Michel Fokine
Music: Camille Saint-Saëns
First performed: Saint Petersburg, 1905

I desire that my message of beauty and joy and life shall be taken up and carried on after me. I hope that when Anna Pavlova is forgotten, the memory of her dancing will live with the people. If I have achieved even that little for my art I am content.—Anna Pavlova

Dying Swan has nothing to do with the ballet *Swan Lake*. It is a short solo piece that was created especially for Anna Pavlova of the Ballets Russes, showing a swan in the last moments of its life. Many ballerinas have performed it since then but it was Pavlova's masterpiece.

There was nothing in her background that suggested Anna would be a great ballerina. She was born premature and sickly in Saint Petersburg in 1881. She grew up poor in a small village, so when her grandmother took her to see a ballet at age eight, it was a special treat. From then on, all she could think about was ballet. Two years later, she auditioned for ballet school and was immediately picked out as a future star.

Incredibly, Anna's most famous solo, the *Dying Swan*, was created in only a few minutes. She and the choreographer, **Michel Fokine**, were friends, and she danced the lead in almost all of his ballets. Fokine liked to play the mandolin. He was playing the Swan music from Camille Saint-Saëns's *Carnival of the Animals* when Anna stopped by to ask him if he would create a solo for her.

He said, "Why not the Swan?"

The *Dying Swan* was part of Anna's life from then on. It is said that her very last words were, "Prepare my Swan costume."

Listen to Track 14
to hear a little bit of the sad swan
music that inspired Fokine.

On her first trip to dance in Stockholm, Anna Pavlova caused such a sensation that after the show, young men took the horses from her carriage so they could drag it back to the hotel themselves!

Sweet Inspiration

Anna Pavlova was the inspiration for another of Michel Fokine's famous ballets. It was originally called *Chopiniana* because it was danced to the music of Chopin. They still call it that in Russia. In most of the world, it is now known as *Les Sylphides* (The Fairies)—but don't confuse it with *La Sylphide*, which you read about already. It was an unusual ballet for its time because it had no story but simply used dance to create a mood.

For a long time *Les Sylphides* was the most widely performed ballet in the world—more popular than *Swan Lake* is today. British audiences loved it so much that there was a tradition that no one should disturb the performance with applause until the very end. Anyone who did clap was loudly shushed!

Firebird

Original choreography: Michel Fokine
Music: Igor Stravinsky
First performed: Paris, 1910 (by the Ballets Russes)

Firebird is based on a Russian folk tale.

Once upon a time, in a snowy birch forest, a young prince named Ivan wakes from a dream. He has just imagined a very beautiful princess and he sets out on a great journey through the woods to find her.

As the sun is going down, he sees a dazzling orange bird, a Firebird. If he can catch it, this magical creature can make the prince's dreams come true.

Listen to Track 15.
This is the theme that plays as the Firebird dances. Can you imagine a brilliant orange bird flying around the stage as you listen to the flute?

Quietly he inches up to the Firebird and pounces. The bird beats its wings and tries to escape, but the prince won't let go. The Firebird finally breaks free, leaving one of its fiery tail feathers in the prince's hand. Even one feather from the great Firebird contains enough magic to protect him.

Still holding on to the feather, the prince comes upon a great castle just as twelve princesses are coming out of the gate. The very last princess is the beautiful girl of the prince's dream! They dance and play together, and Ivan learns that the palace is under the control of an evil sorcerer named Kastchei who is protected by frightening ogres and demons.

Ivan waves the magic feather at the monsters. One by one they back away, but Kastchei is very powerful. He is about to attack Ivan when the Firebird swoops in to the rescue. She drops a golden sword before Ivan and spins around to confuse the monsters. Ivan is able to battle Kastchei and break the spell.

Prince Ivan marries the beautiful princess and they live happily ever after.

The Greatest

In the early part of the twentieth century, two Ballets Russes choreographers, Michel Fokine and **Leonid Massine**, were considered the greatest in the world. They both had many artistic interests. Fokine studied music and painting as well as dance, and Massine thought about becoming an actor.

Fokine, who had made his debut as a dancer with the Imperial Russian Ballet on his eighteenth birthday, created unusual works for the Ballets Russes that were not accepted by the major theaters of Saint Petersburg. He could memorize an entire orchestral score, and he always came to the first rehearsal of a ballet with all of the choreography completely worked out—but he also had a terrible temper. He eventually settled in the United States, and created his last works for American Ballet Theater.

Leonid Massine was hired by Diaghilev to replace Vaslav Nijinsky when he left in 1914. During his career, Massine choreographed more than fifty ballets but was best known for the ones that included folk and character dance. He also choreographed and danced in some movies, including *The Red Shoes*, which you might have seen.

As time went on, Fokine and Massine were overshadowed by **George Balanchine** and **Frederick Ashton** (you'll read more about them later). In fact, although he was one of the most important choreographers of his day, Massine's works are rarely performed anymore.

Petrouchka

Original choreography: Michel Fokine
Music: Igor Stravinsky
First performed: Paris, 1911

It's 1830. The people of Saint Petersburg are gathering in the town square for their traditional celebration just before Lent—something like a Russian Mardi Gras. The crowd is called in to see a puppet show that includes a pretty wind-up ballerina, an exotic Moor (North African) doll, and a sad-looking puppet boy named Petrouchka. Both the Moor and Petrouchka are in love with the ballerina. They begin to fight over her. The man in charge of the puppet show, called the Charlatan (a word that means "faker"), is not pleased.

After the celebration, the Charlatan throws Petrouchka into his room, and to Petrouchka it feels like a prison. He bangs on the door and pounds on the walls, but no one hears him. Poor, trapped Petrouchka!

The whole room seems to brighten a moment later, when the ballerina opens a door and steps

Petrouchka isn't the only ballet about toys coming to life. In fact, there are two more that you have already read about right in this book. Can you remember what they are?

A. *The Nutcracker and Coppélia*

in. Petrouchka is so happy to see her that he leaps and bounces, but the beautiful doll is not impressed. She turns and leaves. Petrouchka crumples sadly to the floor. But then he throws himself against the wall as hard as he can and makes a hole in it. He is free!

When the ballerina visits the Moor, he charms her with a clumsy dance and she perches upon his lap. Petrouchka leaps into the room in an attempt to rescue the ballerina. Once again he and the Moor fight.

In one ballet in 1911, Nijinsky wore a costume all covered in petals so he would look like a rose. They had to keep fixing the costume because his fans stole the petals for souvenirs.

The next day the dolls are supposed to perform at the fair again, but they fight fiercely. This time, the Moor overpowers the little puppet and Petrouchka falls to the ground. His death scene is so convincing that someone calls a policeman, but the Charlatan just laughs, reminding them that Petrouchka is nothing but a puppet. As the Charlatan takes the ragdoll away, his soul rises over the theater and he shakes his fist at his former tyrant—and at anyone else who did not believe he was real.

A Dancer to Remember

You may remember that Vaslav Nijinsky could do more entrechats than any dancer of his time. He could also leap higher than anyone else.

Both of Nijinsky's parents were dancers, and he grew up in the Caucasus region of Russia, dancing with his brother and sister. At the age of nine he began studying at the Imperial School of Dancing in Saint Petersburg.

When he was sixteen, his teachers urged him to leave the school and begin dancing professionally, but he decided to remain with his class. Even before his graduation, he was invited to dance before the czar at his Winter Palace.

As great as he was, Nijinsky seemed to cause trouble wherever he went. He was fired from the Marinsky Theater because of what he wore—or, rather, *didn't* wear—in the ballet *Giselle*. In those days, men usually wore a pair of shorts beneath their jackets but Nijinsky went without them, wearing only tights. This was scandalous in the early 1900s. (Especially with the czar's daughter in the audience!)

After that, he danced full time with Diaghilev's Ballets Russes and did most of his performing outside Russia. The ballets that Nijinsky choreographed for the Ballets Russes were so unusual they actually caused riots.

The French poet Jean Cocteau wrote that Vaslav Nijinsky's dancing was "like some lovely poem written in all capitals."

Unfortunately Nijinsky's career was cut short by mental illness —he stopped dancing at age twenty-nine. He died in London in 1950 and is buried next to a famous dancer you read about earlier, Auguste Vestris, in Paris.

The Rite of Spring

Original choreography: Vaslav Nijinsky
Music: Igor Stravinsky
First performed: Paris, 1913

The Rite of Spring (Le Sacre du Printemps in French) caused quite a stir when it was first shown in Paris. Audiences expecting to see beautiful maidens in flowing white gowns were shocked by Nijinsky's choreography. Instead of using turnout, Nijinsky's dancers performed with their feet in a position that might be called "turn in"—they were pigeon-toed and knock-kneed. Instead of making light, graceful movements, they threw their bodies heavily around the stage.

And then there was the story of the ballet itself. Set in prehistoric Russia, the ballet shows primitive people excitedly choosing and then sacrificing a young woman to the gods—an annual ceremony they hold every spring.

The audience was confused even before the dancers came onstage. Stravinsky's score began with a bassoon solo played so high that people in the audience couldn't tell what instrument it was.

Amid the wealthy ballet fans in the audience were many art students who had been given free tickets by Diaghilev, the producer. As some members of the audience booed and jeered, the students, who loved anything new and different, shouted back at them. There was so much noise

Listen to Track 16.
Even the music of this revolutionary ballet confused audiences. This part is called "The Dance of the Earth." It sounds more like a bunch of giants stomping around than like ballet music, doesn't it?

that the dancers couldn't hear the music, and Nijinsky was forced to call out the time for them.

The ballet was performed only six times before it closed for good.

On the first night that The Rite of Spring *was performed, composer Camille Saint-Saëns stormed out of the theater. (Remember? He was the one who wrote* Carnival of the Animals, *which includes the music of the* Dying Swan.*)*

Peter and the Wolf

Original choreography: Adolph Bolm
Music: Sergei Prokofiev
First performed: San Francisco, 1940

In Prokofiev's very special symphony, each character is represented by one instrument of the orchestra. If you are familiar with the instruments then maybe you can understand how a bassoon might sound like a grandfather or a clarinet like a cat. Peter's theme is played by a string quartet—and when you hear the thundering beat of timpani (kettledrums), it means the hunters are coming.

The story of *Peter and the Wolf* goes like this. One summer day a boy named Peter is walking through a meadow when he meets a bird and a duck. He notices a cat sneaking toward the bird. "Look out!" he shouts as the cat is about to pounce—and the bird flies away.

In 1935, Natalya Sats, the founder of the Moscow Theater for Children, hired the composer **Sergei Prokofiev** (sair-gay pro-KOF-ee-yev) to create a special symphony that would help teach children about the different instruments in the orchestra. Prokofiev came up with *Peter and the Wolf*, in which each character is represented by a particular instrument and theme. Four years later, in America, it was turned into a ballet.

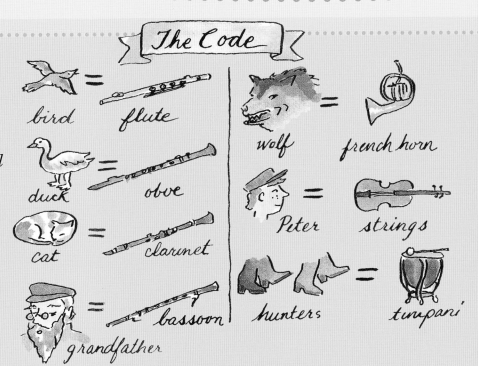

The Code

bird = flute

duck = oboe

cat = clarinet

grandfather = bassoon

wolf = french horn

Peter = strings

hunters = timpani

Peter's grandfather pulls Peter back through the gate just as a wolf comes near. The bird spies the wolf and starts to chirp so that the cat wakes up

Listen to Track 17.
This music represents the cat. How does it compare to the cat theme from *Sleeping Beauty* that you heard in Track 10?

and climbs a tree—but the duck isn't fast enough to get away, so the wolf gulps him down!

Peter runs out with a rope and tries to catch the wolf. He climbs the tree and inches out onto a limb. He asks the bird to fly around the wolf's head and distract him—but warns the bird to be very careful not to get caught.

Peter makes a loop with the rope and manages to catch the wolf by the tail.

Just then some hunters come out of the woods. They start shooting at the wolf but Peter calls out, "Don't shoot! Let's take him to the zoo!" Peter, along with the hunters, his grandfather, the bird, and the cat, parade the wolf down the street.

Romeo and Juliet

Original choreography: Leonid Lavrovsky
Music: Sergei Prokofiev
First performed: Leningrad, 1940

Tchaikovsky began composing music for a ballet about Shakespeare's famous lovers, Romeo and Juliet, but he died before he could complete it. Fortunately, another Russian composer, Peter and the Wolf's Prokofiev, set the story to music instead, and it is now considered one of the most beautiful classic ballets.

This sad love story takes place in Verona, Italy, where two powerful families, the Montagues and Capulets, have been enemies for years. One night, young Romeo Montague and his friends Mercutio and Benvolio decide to sneak into a party hosted by the Capulets.

At the party Romeo spots a beautiful young woman and asks her to dance. He doesn't realize that she is Juliet Capulet, daughter of his sworn enemy and promised in marriage to a man named Paris. Romeo and Juliet fall in love at first sight.

Romeo can't stop thinking of Juliet, so he comes to the courtyard below her balcony and they admit their love to each other. They are married secretly by a local clergyman, Friar Laurence.

Things become more complicated for the couple. Juliet's cousin, Tybalt, challenges Mercutio to a duel and kills him. Romeo chases after Tybalt and kills him with his own sword. The prince of Verona banishes Romeo from the city but he goes to Juliet one last time before he must leave forever.

Juliet rushes to Friar Laurence, and tells him the whole story. He comes up with a plan to reunite the couple. He gives Juliet a sleeping potion that will make it seem as if she is dead. The plan is that

Have you heard the famous line "Romeo, Romeo, wherefore art thou Romeo?" Juliet says it in the balcony scene of Shakespeare's play. Juliet isn't asking where Romeo is. "Wherefore" is the way people in Shakespeare's day said, "Why?" Juliet is saying "WHY are you Romeo, my family's enemy?"

Perfect Partners

When a man and a woman dance a duet together it is called a **pas de deux** (pah-de-DERH), which means "step of two" in French.

It may seem as if the man is doing all the work when he lifts a ballerina over his head, but **partnering** takes real teamwork. If the ballerina does not position her body correctly then she is impossible to lift. But if both partners get it right, a male dancer can even hold his partner in the air with just one hand. Teamwork, trust, and concentration are the key.

The famous ballerina **Margot Fonteyn** (MAR-go fon-TAYN) was once asked whether she was in favor of the women's liberation movement. She replied, "Not if it means I have to carry the male dancers instead of them carrying me!"

she will fake her own death and her family will place her in their tomb. The friar will send word to Romeo that she is sleeping there, so Romeo will know to sneak in and wake her up, and then they can run away together.

Juliet drinks the potion as planned, but everything goes wrong. Romeo hears that she is dead but never gets the friar's message that it is not really true. He goes to the tomb and, when he sees his young wife lying there, he is so upset that he takes poison himself. Juliet wakes up to find her Romeo dead beside her. In grief, she takes his knife and ends her own life.

When the Montagues and Capulets see the tragic scene they vow to end their feud forever.

Dance magazine called it **"the most eagerly awaited curtain time in American theatrical history."** It was April 16, 1959, when Russia's Bolshoi Ballet played in the United States for the first time, at the Metropolitan Opera House in New York City. Ballet fans waited outside for thirty-nine hours just to see ballerina **Galina Ulanova** perform *Romeo and Juliet.*

From Russia to America

So far, we've talked about Russia, France, and England but we have barely mentioned the United States. Today, there are great ballet companies in America, including American Ballet Theater, the New York City Ballet, and the Alvin Ailey Company in New York, the Joffrey Ballet in Chicago, and the San Francisco Ballet. But before the late twentieth century, there was very little home-grown ballet in this country. Of course, people danced here. Great dancers performed on Broadway and in Hollywood movies, and people loved to do all kinds of social dancing, from square dances to the fox trot to the Charleston. But when it came to ballet, Americans had to make do with occasional touring troupes from Europe and Russia.

That all began to change when a man named George Balanchine came to America. Balanchine had been a dancer with the Ballets Russes, but when Diaghilev died he decided it was time to form his own company. As a ballet master,

Tappa-Tap!

Tap!

A Real Toe Tapper

In the 1920s and '30s, ballet was not yet popular in the United States, but American audiences were fascinated by "toe dancing." Novelty performers of the day combined pointe work with all kinds of acrobatics and crazy stunts. A popular oddity was "toe-tapping." Dancers performed en pointe with metal taps on their shoes. One of the most famous toe-tappers was Harriet Hoctor, "America's Most Cleverest Ballerina." Harriet once tapped up and down an escalator in pointe-tap shoes—not a trick that you should try anytime soon!

Balanchine had always been on the lookout for wealthy investors to support the company, and that is how he met an American ballet fan, **Lincoln Kirstein**, who suggested that Balanchine come to America.

Balanchine had seen the great **Fred Astaire** and **Ginger Rogers** in the movies, and he thought there must be people who could become great ballet dancers in America. In 1934, he founded the School of American Ballet in New York City, along with the dance company that would become the New York City Ballet.

He created many interesting new ballets and restaged many classics. In fact, it is thanks to Balanchine that *The Nutcracker* is a holiday tradition in the United States. Yet he is best known for creating ballets without stories. "You put a man and a woman onstage together and already it's a story," he once said.

THE YOUNGEST BALLERINA

Suzanne Farrell was the youngest ballerina in the history of the New York City Ballet. George Balanchine called her his muse (inspiration), but she might never have danced at all if she hadn't been bored sitting in the car during her sister's ballet class.

Suzanne was a tomboy. She liked to climb trees and play dodgeball, and being a ballerina never entered her mind. But one day she wandered into her older sister's dance class and the ballet teacher invited her to join.

She liked dance right away but preferred tap and jazz to ballet. She didn't start studying ballet seriously until she was twelve, which makes it even more amazing that she auditioned for George Balanchine at age fifteen. Within a year, she was a member of his company.

Critics have called her the greatest dancer of the twentieth century.

Rodeo

Original choreography: Agnes DeMille
Music: Aaron Copland
First performed: New York, 1942

A ballet called *Rodeo* sounds like fun, doesn't it? And what could be more American? Here's the story.

It is Saturday afternoon on the Burnt Ranch, and time for the weekly rodeo. A tomboy cowgirl hitches up her breeches, ready to join in, but the cowboys won't let a girl compete.

Secretly the cowgirl is in love with the head wrangler, but he pays no attention to her. Instead he flirts with the women in fancy dresses who come to watch the rodeo. The jealous cowgirl rides off and returns on a bucking bronco. Surely this will impress everyone! But the ladies just laugh at the sight and the men ignore her.

The head wrangler invites the rancher's daughter, who is a dressed prettily in ribbons and bows, to the Saturday dance.

At the dance, the cowgirl sits alone. When the boys choose their dancing partners, they all pass her by. Eventually, a champion roper sits by her and tells her that if she wants to attract the attention of the cowboys she should dress a little better. He tries to fix her up but as he does, she sees the wrangler with the rancher's daughter and she runs away in tears. The roper follows her.

The cowgirl decides to try something new and she returns in a bright red dress. This time, she captures the attention of all the boys—including the wrangler. He and the roper fight over her but in the end she decides to stay with the roper, who cared for her even when she wore pants.

> After the success of *Rodeo*, Richard Rodgers and Oscar Hammerstein invited Agnes de Mille to choreograph their new Broadway musical, *Oklahoma!* She went on to become one of America's most prominent choreographers. One of her great ideas was putting a "dream ballet" or "story ballet" into her musicals, a dance piece that helped reveal what the characters were thinking and feeling.

Fancy Free

Choreography: Jerome Robbins
Music: Leonard Bernstein
First performed: New York, 1944

Fancy Free was the first ballet created by Jerome Robbins. It surprised people because it was set in the present time, not "once upon a time," and audiences instantly loved it.

The story is simple. Three sailors are on leave in New York when they spot a beautiful woman. Two of them take off after her, and the third stays behind and meets another woman. He tells her some war stories to impress her and it seems to work—he gets to dance with her. Then his two friends come back with the first woman.

> **Fancy Free** *inspired a musical about sailors called* **On the Town**, *which became a famous movie starring Gene Kelly and Frank Sinatra.*

ONE WAY

Now there are three men and only two women, so the sailors decide to have a dancing contest to impress the women.

The dance contest turns into an argument. The sailors get so caught up in fighting one another that they don't even notice when the women wander away.

The three men pick themselves up, dust themselves off, and vow they will never let a woman come between them again. But…just then they see another beautiful woman and they all turn and follow her!

Ballet to Broadway

Fancy Free was the first ballet choreographed by **Jerome Robbins**, who would go on to create many great ballets, Broadway musicals, and movie dance sequences. He was the son of a poor delicatessen owner, and grew up studying all kinds of dance, from ballet and modern to Spanish. He used all of these styles to create ballets that are considered distinctly American.

Robbins made his debut with the Yiddish Art Theater in 1937 and worked as a song-and-dance man at a resort hotel before working on Broadway. *Fancy Free* premiered when he was only twenty-five and everyone wanted to hire him, but Robbins preferred ballet to Broadway. He admired George Balanchine so much that he joined the New York City Ballet to work with him, but he was better known for such musicals as *West Side Story.* He co-directed the movie version of this and won an Oscar for it. He also created one of the most famous dances on screen—the bottle dance in *Fiddler on the Roof*—in which a line of men dance with wine bottles on the top of their heads and never spill a drop.

Wallace Muro, a dancer who performed in *Fiddler on the Roof* on Broadway said, "There was a rule about the bottle dance. Periodically one of the dancers had to drop his bottle….Jerry Robbins wanted it to be exciting. He felt that the audience needed to understand that those bottles weren't glued on—they were really balanced."

Circus Polka

Choreography: George Balanchine
Music: Igor Stravinsky
First performed: New York, 1942

When you think of ballet, what animal comes to mind? A swan maybe?

What about ELEPHANTS?

In 1942, the Barnum and Bailey Circus hired George Balanchine to create one of the most unusual ballets ever. *The Circus Polka* was performed entirely by elephants—real, live elephants!

When Balanchine got the assignment he immediately called his friend Igor Stravinsky and asked him to compose the music.

"What kind of music?" asked Stravinsky.

"A polka."

"For whom?"

"Elephants."

"How old?"

"Young."

"If they are very young, I'll do it!" he said.

The star was a "ballerina" named Modoc. The newspaper said, "Modoc the elephant danced with amazing grace, and in time to the tune, closing in perfect cadence with the crashing finale."

The elephant ballet was performed 425 times—that's 419 more than another Stravinsky ballet that you've already read about, *The Rite of Spring*.

In 1972, Jerome Robbins created a new circus ballet for (human) dance students and an adult ringmaster, using the same Stravinsky music.

Believe it or not, Circus Polka was not the first ballet performed by animals. A "horse ballet" was part of the wedding celebration for France's King Louis XIII. In that one, twenty-one horses "danced" in feathered costumes.

Cinderella

Original choreography: Rostislav Zakharov
Music: Sergei Prokofiev
First performed: Moscow, 1945

I bet you already know the story of *Cinderella*. It has been a favorite fairy tale for hundreds of years, and for more than two hundred years choreographers have been making ballets based on it. This is the most famous one.

Cinderella sits by the fire as her ugly stepsisters get ready for the prince's ball. It will be the finest party in the land, but poor Cinderella has not been invited. When a strange old woman comes to the door, the stepsisters are rude to her, but kind Cinderella offers her some bread. It isn't until the stepsisters have left for the ball that the old woman reveals herself to be a fairy godmother.

With a wave of her magic wand, the fairy godmother changes a pumpkin into a luxurious coach, and Cinderella's rags into a beautiful gown. She waves to Cinderella as she leaves for the ball, but warns her that the magic spell will last only until midnight.

Cinderella is the loveliest woman at the ball, and the Prince falls in love with her.

Everyone knows the story of Cinderella! There may be as many as 1,500 versions of the story from all over the world. Here is how they say "Cinderella" in some other countries. France: Cendrillon (sahn-dree-OHN); Germany: Aschenbrödel (OSH-en-bro-del); Russia: Zolushka (zo-LOOSH-ka).

They dance together but suddenly the clock strikes midnight. Cinderella runs away so quickly that she leaves one of her slippers behind.

The Prince must find the beautiful girl from the ball! He goes from house to house trying to find the girl whose foot fits the tiny and beautiful shoe.

When he arrives at Cinderella's house, the ugly stepsisters push Cinderella aside, and each tries to force her own foot into the shoe. No luck, of course. Then Cinderella steps forward. A small shoe slips from her pocket and the Prince recognizes it immediately. It is the match for the one he is carrying! She and the Prince are soon married and live happily ever after.

Ugly, Indeed!

In England and America the ugly stepsisters are often danced by men in women's dresses so they will look comical and physically ugly. In Russia, they are played by real ballerinas and only their behavior is ugly—not their faces.

Daphnis and Chloë

Choreography: Frederick Ashton
Music: Maurice Ravel
First performed: London, 1951

Magical Pan

You may have seen pictures of the Greek god known as Pan. In mythology, he was born with the legs and horns of a goat, and was a shepherd and protector of all flocks. He played a shepherd's pipe that he invented, made of bound reeds, and (just like in the ballet) was known for scaring people, especially when they were in lonely places. That is where we get the word "panic," and James Barrie surely had him in mind when he named Peter Pan.

Here is how the story goes. Daphnis and Chloë live on a warm island in the Mediterranean Sea. Daphnis is a handsome young shepherd. He and Chloë have been friends since they were children, and have fallen deeply in love.

One night, as Daphnis sleeps, a band of pirates invades the island and, before Daphnis can do anything, the pirate's leader, Bryaxis, kidnaps Chloë and carries her away. Daphnis prays to the god Pan to bring Chloë back to him.

On the pirates' island, Bryaxis forces Chloë to dance for him. She begs him to let her go but he only laughs. Suddenly, lightning strikes and the goat-footed god Pan appears! Bryaxis trembles with fear and orders the pirates to let Chloë go.

Chloe returns to Daphnis. He is so happy to see her that they dance together as Pan plays his magic reed flute.

*The mythological story of **Daphnis and Chloë** was first made into a ballet in 1912 by the Ballets Russes, but the British version is the most famous.*

Listen to Track 18.
Now that you know a little bit about Pan, does this haunting, magical flute music seem to suit his personality?

Ballet All-Stars

The English choreographer **Frederick Ashton** created *Daphnis and Chloë* for a great British ballerina, Margot Fonteyn. She started dancing with an English ballet company when she was only fourteen, as a snowflake in *The Nutcracker*. In just two years, she moved up to leading roles.

At first, Ashton and Fonteyn had trouble getting along. He said her feet were too soft, "like pats of butter." She thought he was too strict and demanding. Fortunately, they grew to like and respect each other, and Ashton created many great ballets for her.

Fonteyn was also famous for playing roles in classical ballets, including *Sleeping Beauty*. In 1954, when she was thirty-five, she was knighted and became Dame Margot Fonteyn.

In 1960, at an age when most ballerinas are ready to retire, she was paired with a young dance sensation named **Rudolf Nureyev** (nur-AY-ev). They couldn't have been more different. She was nineteen years older. She was cool and classical. He was athletic, fiery, and temperamental. Yet, somehow the pairing worked.

Fonteyn kept dancing until she was well into her fifties, an incredibly long career for a dancer. She even danced the part of fourteen-year-old Juliet when she was forty-six!

Audiences flocked to see Fonteyn and Nureyev. At one performance of Swan Lake *in Austria, they set a world record for the most curtain calls ever recorded in ballet: eighty-nine!*

Rudolf Nureyev was one of the greatest dancers of the twentieth century, and his life story proves that you don't need to be rich or live in a big city to succeed as a dancer.

He was born in 1938, on a moving train somewhere in Siberia. Rudolf and his family lived in a tiny apartment that they shared with another family, and they often had nothing but boiled potatoes to eat.

In 1945, he and his sisters snuck in to see the Bashkir Opera and Ballet Theater, and Rudolf knew then and there what he wanted to do with his life. He learned the basics of ballet in his hometown of Ufa, but dancing with a great Russian ballet company was still a distant dream. The great ballet schools were in Leningrad and Moscow, a thousand miles away.

By the time Rudolf made it to Leningrad, he was seventeen. Most students were graduating at that age, not starting. "Young man," said one teacher, "you'll either become a brilliant dancer or a total failure—and most likely you'll be a failure." He managed to study with one of the school's most famous teachers, and three years later he was offered a contract with the Kirov Ballet. After three more years, while he was on tour in Paris, Rudolf "defected," meaning that he stopped living in the Soviet Union. He wanted to live someplace where he had more opportunities as an artist and as a person. He moved permanently to Paris and soon became one of the biggest dance stars in the world. He also choreographed a number of ballets, such as his own versions of *Don Quixote* and *Romeo and Juliet.*

Rudolf Nureyev was once on *The Muppet Show*. He sang a duet with Miss Piggy and danced *Swine Lake* with a giant pig!

KNIGHT OF BALLET

British ballet did not really exist when Frederick Ashton was a boy. Growing up in Peru, South America, Ashton saw the beautiful ballerina Anna Pavlova and became intrigued with her—and with ballet in general. When he was a teenager, in the 1920s, he came to London with almost no money and a dream of becoming a dancer. He went on to become one of the greatest choreographers of the century, and helped establish ballet in England.

In the United States, choreographers such as George Balanchine were moving away from ballets that told stories, but Ashton and other English choreographers created many new story ballets. Ashton even made a ballet film of the tales of Beatrix Potter, in which dancers in lifelike masks played the many different animals in her stories.

"Ashton has a way of using dance so it appears to be the only natural form of communication," wrote Margot Fonteyn, who starred in some of Ashton's greatest ballets. "His movements are often more expressive than words."

Ashton was made a knight in 1962, so he is known as *Sir* Frederick Ashton.

The Painter Who Loved Ballet

Have you seen a beautiful painting of ballerinas stretching and lacing up their shoes, or a statue of a little ballerina? It was probably done by an artist named **Edgar Degas**. He was fascinated by ballet and spent many hours watching it and visiting the ballerinas backstage. He became one of the most important artists of the 19th century. When people first saw his most famous sculpture, "Little Dancer, Aged Fourteen," they hated it! It was made of wax, with real clothes and hair! It looked so much like a real girl that they were startled—it didn't seem like art to them. Degas hid it away but after he died it was cast in bronze and displayed at museums around the world.

BALLET STAR

If you know the name of only one ballet dancer, chances are it is Mikhail Baryshnikov. He was born in 1948 in Riga, Latvia, which was part of the then–Soviet Union.

Like another late-starter, Nureyev, when Baryshnikov began his dance training at age fifteen, some people thought he was already too old. They also thought that he was too short (five foot seven) and even too boyish-looking to land leading roles. But he was so good that it didn't take long for him to change people's minds. He joined the Kirov Ballet and was given solo roles immediately. Most dancers have to spend some time in the background, but not Baryshnikov.

He was enjoying great success but, at that time in the Soviet Union, dancers were limited in the types of dance they could perform. He wanted to explore everything from classic ballet to modern dance and Broadway, so when the Kirov was touring in Canada, Baryshnikov stayed behind and defected, becoming a member of the National Ballet of Canada. He later became an American citizen and worked with the American Ballet Theater and the New York City Ballet.

He was America's first huge ballet star, famous for his breathtaking leaps and original takes on traditional steps. Even people who know nothing about ballet have heard his name. He has been in several movies, including *The Turning Point* and *White Nights*. He even has his own line of dancewear and a perfume called "Baryshnikov"!

The Little Humpbacked Horse

Choreography: Alexander Radunsky
Music: Rodion Shchedrin
First performed: Moscow, 1959

This is a colorful and comical tale about a Russian boy named Ivan who lives on a farm in the country with his father and two older brothers. His brothers think Ivan is a fool and they never include him in anything they do, but Ivan is always happy and kind to them anyway.

One night, their father sends the two older brothers out to watch the field because someone has been stealing the corn. Instead of acting as guards they drink and fall asleep.

> **This is one of the first ballets based on a Russian folk story, and is also known as The Czar Maiden.**

Ivan finds them there. As he is covering them with a blanket he sees an enchanted white horse leaping across the sky. He tries to capture her by grabbing her tail. The horse begs Ivan to let her go free and, when he does, she gives him a gift of three horses. Two are beautiful golden steeds and the third is a tiny humpbacked horse. The magical white horse explains to Ivan that he can sell the big horses if he wants to, but he must always keep the little humpbacked horse at his side and she will be his friend forever.

Just then a golden firebird flies overhead and drops a feather. The little humpbacked horse warns Ivan not to pick it up because it is bad luck, but he doesn't listen. As he chases the feather, his brothers wake up and steal the big horses. They take them to a market outside the palace of the czar (king).

Ivan's brothers are selling the horses to the czar when Ivan finds them. The czar is having trouble controlling his new horses. Ivan easily tames them. The czar is so impressed that he makes Ivan the chief of the royal stables. The czar's assistant, the Gentleman of the Bedchamber, gets very jealous and decides to find a way to get rid of Ivan.

The Gentleman finds Ivan's feather in the stable and reports it to the czar, figuring that this will get Ivan in trouble. It does, but not in the way the Gentleman hopes. The czar is fascinated by the feather. He touches it to a painting of birds, and they come to life. He touches it to a painting of a beautiful woman, the Queen Maiden, and she, too, comes to life—though she quickly disappears.

The Gentleman convinces the czar that only Ivan can find the Queen Maiden (thinking that it will be impossible and Ivan will never come back). The czar sends Ivan on a journey and with the help of the little humpbacked horse he finds the Queen Maiden. They dance together and fall in love.

When the czar sees the lady from his painting he asks her to marry him. Because he is the czar she cannot say no. Instead, she stalls him—she throws her ring into the ocean and says that she will not marry him until the ring is found. The czar calls upon the only person he knows can perform impossible tasks—Ivan—and once again he and the horse head out on a journey, this time to the bottom of the ocean, where they meet fish and water sprites who help them find the ring.

Ivan returns the ring. The Queen Maiden is happy to see him but unhappy to see the ring. She does not want to marry the czar, she wants to marry Ivan! So she tells the czar that she will only marry him if he can make himself young again by jumping into a giant pot of boiling milk. The czar says he will do it, but he wants Ivan to try it first. The little humpbacked horse protects him once more: Ivan jumps in and is transformed into a handsome prince.

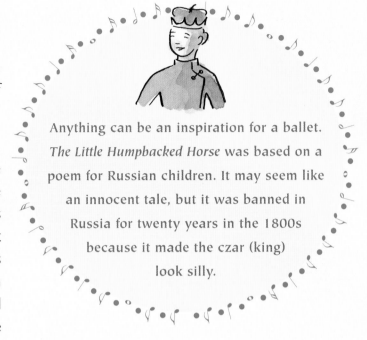

Anything can be an inspiration for a ballet. *The Little Humpbacked Horse* was based on a poem for Russian children. It may seem like an innocent tale, but it was banned in Russia for twenty years in the 1800s because it made the czar (king) look silly.

The czar immediately throws off his cape and crown and leaps into the pot—but the little horse's magic doesn't work for him and he never comes out.

Ivan, the Queen Maiden, and the little humpbacked horse live happily ever after.

A Midsummer Night's Dream

Original choreogaphy: George Balanchine
Music: Felix Mendelssohn
First performed: New York, 1962

Oberon, the king of the fairies, and his queen, Titania, are arguing, and Oberon wants to embarrass her. Oberon orders a sprite named Puck to find a flower that has been shot by Cupid's arrow and to bring it to him. While Titania sleeps, Oberon sprinkles the magic juice from the flower on her, knowing that it will make her fall in love with whoever she sees when she wakes up.

Elsewhere in the woods, a young girl named Helena is crying because she is in love with Demetrius but he does not love her back. Oberon orders Puck to use the magic of the flower on Demetrius so he will fall in love with Helena. But at the same time, another young couple, Hermia and Lysander, are walking in the forest. Puck mistakes Lysander for Demetrius, and sprinkles the liquid on the wrong boy. The first person Lysander sees is Helena—the wrong girl—and he falls head-over-heels in love with her. When Hermia finds him he has no interest in her at all. Helena is confused...she does not love Lysander. The lovers are all mixed up!

When Puck realizes what he has done, he tries to make things right by using the flower on Demetrius, who also falls in love with Helena, the wrong girl—so now the two men are fighting over Helena, and poor Hermia is left alone.

As all this is going on, a group of amateur actors is wandering through the woods. Oberon decides to make his joke on Titania even better. He has Puck change Bottom-the-weaver into a donkey. Titania, who has been sprinkled with the flower juice, wakes up and thinks Bottom is the most beautiful being she has ever seen. Once Oberon has had his fun, he releases Titania from the spell and she is ashamed that she had cuddled up to a donkey!

Now Puck must try to fix the damage he has caused the young couples in the woods. He steers the two men in different directions and they both get lost. Eventually they get tired and fall asleep. When they wake up the couples are all sorted out and they decide to have a double wedding—with lots of dancing, of course.

You have already read about one ballet based on a Shakespeare play, Romeo and Juliet. The composer Felix Mendelssohn wrote music for another one, A Midsummer Night's Dream. Years later George Balanchine was inspired by the music to create a ballet. The only problem was—there wasn't enough music, so Balanchine added some other Mendelssohn pieces.

One night in Athens...

Puck

Listen to Track 19.
This is the music from the couples' wedding. Have you heard this music at weddings before? Mendelssohn's Wedding March is still the most popular music at weddings. This part of the wedding is called the "recessional."

Oberon

Titania

Bottom-
The Weaver

Helena   Demetrius   Hermia   Lysander

That Special Spark

Dancers spend a lot of time training their hips to turn out, their toes to work in pointe shoes, and their arms to stay in the right positions. But, besides all of those skills, true ballet stars need to have a little bit of magic, too.

Once, a nine-year-old ballet student asked Russian ballet dancer Valery Lantratov whether the arms or the legs were more important in dance. "Neither," he answered. "The most important is the head; the head and the ears, because first, dancing is mental. The head sends the signals to the ears that they have to hear the music, and the ears

La Fille Mal Gardée   La Sylphide   Coppélia

send the signal to the arms and legs on how to move, and then of course the eyes, because they have a dancer's spark, light up with the specific light of learning."

Now you know a little bit more about ballet—about the famous dancers, choreographers, and composers, and the stories they bring to life on the stage. You've done a few dance steps and listened to some great ballet music. You've imagined what it is like to be a great dancer and to sit in the dark watching a marvelous ballet. Maybe you have even discovered the "dancer's spark" in yourself! Now it is up to you. Do you want to study ballet, even though it can be hard work? Do you want to watch live ballet on the stage? Wherever you live you can probably explore both of those things, because, thanks to all of the great artists and works in this book, ballet is everywhere. Enjoy!

Sleeping Beauty   Don Quixote   Cinderella   Peter and the Wolf   Daphnis and Chloé

Glossary

Arabesque A pose on one leg with the other extended straight behind the body.

Attitude Standing on one leg with the other bent at the knee and extended in front or behind the body. Dancers like to joke about ballerinas having "attitude."

Ballerina A female ballet dancer. There is no equivalent for male dancers—we just call them "ballet dancers" or, in French, "danseurs."

Barre A horizontal bar used for ballet practice.

Battement Tendu An exercise in which one foot slides forward, backward, or to the side along the floor.

Choreographer A person who creates and directs the movements of a dance.

Class A series of movements and stretches to prepare the body for dance.

Classic Tutu A ballet dress whose short skirt, built of layers of stiff tulle, sticks straight out.

Composer A person who creates music.

Demi Pointe Literally, "half pointe," balanced on the balls of the feet, with the heels raised high.

Développé A slow movement in which the leg is gradually extended to the highest possible point. (The height "develops.")

Divertissements Entertaining "diversions" or time-outs from the main story of a story ballet.

Entrechat A vertical jump during which the dancer repeatedly crosses the feet and beats them together.

Five Classical Positions The basic five placements for a dancer's feet.

Fouetté The French word for "whip," a quick whipping movement of the leg followed by a pirouette or spin.

Impressario A theatrical producer who hires and presents entertainers

Jeté A leap made from one foot to the other.

Mythological Based on a myth or legend.

Partnering Two dancers helping each other perform movements, such as in a pas de deux.

Pas de Deux A duet, or "dance for two" within a ballet. There is also a pas de trois, which is a dance for three; and a pas de quatre, a dance for four.

Pirouette A spin on the tips of the toes or the ball of the foot.

Plié A bend of the knee or knees.

Pointe Shoes Shoes with specially stiffened tips, made for dancing on the tips of the toes.

Romantic Ballet A fantasy or fairy-tale ballet set in an imaginary world.

Romantic Tutu A tutu with a calf-length skirt made of soft layers of tulle.

Soloist A dancer who dances alone. The people who dance divertissements or individual characters other than the lead are "soloists."

Tulle Fine netting used to make the skirts of tutus.

Turnout In ballet the legs, and feet must be swiveled outward, starting from the hips, to face sideways.

Tutu A style of costume for female ballet dancers, with a fitted bodice and stiff or fluffy skirt. (See classic tutu and romantic tutu.)

Learn More About It

There are lots of other great books about ballet. Here are a few to get you started—and be sure to ask your librarian for more ideas.

If you want to be a ballerina...

Ballet Class for Beginners. DVD. Kultur, 1986.

Bray-Moffat, Naia, and David Hanley. *Ballet School*. New York: Dorling Kindersley, 2003.

Bussell, Darcey. *The Young Dancer*. London: Dorling Kinserley, 1994.
This book is by a famous English ballerina. She'll tell you all about ballet positions and history.

Ellison, Nancy, and Susan Jaffe. *Becoming a Ballerina*. New York: Universe Publishing, 2003.
Former American Ballet Theatre principal dancer Susan Jaffe tells you all about being a ballerina.

Friedman, Lisa, and K. C. Bailey. *First Lessons in Ballet*. New York: Workman Publishing, 1999.

Mara, Thalia. *Steps in Ballet*. Princeton: Princeton Book Company, 2004.
Thalia Mara was a ballerina in Europe and started a famous ballet school in New York. She offers great tips for young dancers.

If you want to read more about the great ballets...

Geras, Adele, and Emma Chichester Clark. *The Magic of the Ballet: Swan Lake*. Gullane Children's Books, 2001.

Hoffmann, E. T. A. *Nutcracker*. New York: Gramercy Books, 1984.
This is the original story on which they based the ballet. It has scenes that you won't see on stage.

Kain, Karen. *The Nutcracker*. New York: Tundra Books, 2005.

Canada's renowned prima ballerina, Karen Kain, tells the story of the National Ballet of Canada's production of The Nutcracker.

Newman, Barbara. *The Illustrated Book of Ballet Stories*. New York: DK Publishing, 1997.

Schubert, Leda. *Ballet of the Elephants*. Roaring Brook Press, 2006.

Verdy, Violette. *Of Swans, Sugarplums and Satin Slippers: Ballet Stories for Children*. New York: Scholastic, 1996.

Vagin, Vladimir. *Peter and the Wolf*. New York: Scholastic, 2003.

If you want to read more about famous dancers...

Maybarduk, Linda. *The Dancer Who Flew: A Memoir of Rudolf Nureyev*. Plattsburgh, NY: Tundra Books, 1999.

Pavlova, Anna. *I Dreamed I Was a Ballerina*. New York: Atheneum, 2001.
The famous ballerina Anna Pavlova wrote a charming story about the first time she saw a ballet. And the pictures were created by Edgar Degas!

Reich, Susannah. *José: Born to Dance*. New York: Simon and Schuster, 2005.
This is the story of Mexican-born American dance star José Limón, who gave the world his own kind of dance.

Tallchief, Maria. *Tallchief: America's Prima Ballerina*. New York: Puffin Books, 2001.
Native-American Maria Tallchief, one of the most prominent American ballerinas, wrote her own story just for young people.

If you like made-up stories about dancing...

Holabird, Katherine. *Angelina's Ballet Class*. Grosset & Dunlap, 2006.

Littlesugar, Amy. *Marie in Fourth Position: The Story of Degas' "The Little Dancer."* New York: Philomel, 1996.
Remember reading about Degas? This is a tale about a shy girl who became a model for one of the artist's famous sculptures.

Sweeny, Joan, and Leslie Wu. *Bijou, Bonbon and Beau*. San Francisco: Chronicle, 2002.

CD Track List

Track 1	Michael Praetorius: "Ballet des Baccanales"
Track 2	Erik Satie: "3 Gnossiennes: Lent"
Track 3	Adolphe Adam: "Entrée de Giselle" from *Giselle*
Track 4	Léo Delibes: "Mazurka" from *Coppélia*
Track 5	Léo Delibes: "Musique des automates" from *Coppélia*
Track 6	Aram Khachaturian: "Sabre Dance" from *Gayane*
Track 7	Leon Minkus: "Kitri Enters" from *Don Quixote*
Track 8	Peter Ilyich Tchaikovsky: "By a Lake" from *Swan Lake*
Track 9	Peter Ilyich Tchaikovsky: "In the Castle of Prince Siegfried" from *Swan Lake*
Track 10	Peter Ilyich Tchaikovsky: "Le chat botte et la chatte blanche" from *Sleeping Beauty*
Track 11	Peter Ilyich Tchaikovsky: "L'Oiseau Bleu et la Princesse Florine" from *Sleeping Beauty*
Track 12	Peter Ilyich Tchaikovsky: "Divertissement (Chinese variation)" from *The Nutcracker*
Track 13	Peter Ilyich Tchaikovsky: "Divertissement (Sugar Plum Fairy)" from *The Nutcracker*
Track 14	Camille Saint-Saëns: "Swan" from *Carnival of the Animals*
Track 15	Igor Stravinsky: "Variation de l'oiseau de feu" from *Firebird*
Track 16	Igor Stravinsky: "Le sacrifice" from *The Rite of Spring*
Track 17	Sergei Prokofiev: "The Cat" from *Peter and the Wolf*
Track 18	Maurice Ravel: "Lever du jour" from *Daphnis and Chloë*
Track 19	Felix Mendelssohn: "Wedding March" from *A Midsummer Night's Dream*

Photo Credits